D1614987

STEAM
IN THE
EAST
MIDLANDS

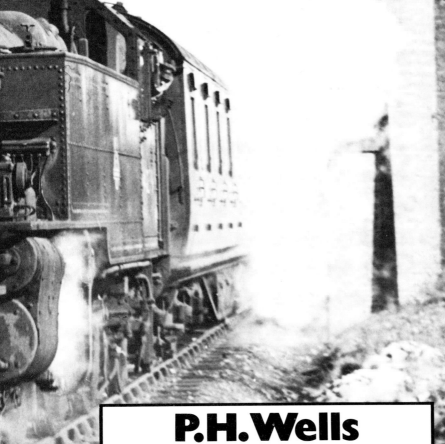

STEAM
IN THE
EAST
MIDLANDS

P.H. Wells

LONDON

IAN ALLAN LTD

First published 1985

ISBN 0 7110 1479 5

© Ian Allan Ltd 1985

Published by Ian Allan Ltd, Shepperton, Surrey;
and printed by Ian Allan Printing Ltd at their works
at Coombelands in Runnymede, England

Introduction

I will begin this introduction with two borrowed quotations:

'For pleasure, Whose? – Mine.'

'I make no pretence to any expert knowledge about the works of a steam locomotive nor the working of a railway.'

These words illustrate exactly the motivation behind this book and the taking of the photographs herein. They are the words of the late Bishop Eric Treacy who, as Canon Treacy, published them in the introduction to a photographic album of his railway photographs over 30 years ago. The book was titled *Steam Up* and it was this, together with the published works of others in an elite band of railway photographers of those days, which inspired me and others like me to try to emulate their skill and artistry with the camera.

However, whilst the contents of *Steam Up* ranged countrywide this album concentrates on an area eastward of a line about 60 miles long drawn from Northampton up to Derby and on the cross-country lines radiating eastwards from the rail centres thereon. I have only featured the northbound trunk routes of the old Great Central, Midland and Great Northern Railways at places where they are intersected by these lines. To complete the picture I have also included the northbound main lines of the Midland to Nottingham from Glendon South Junction near Kettering, the GN/GE joint line from March to Lincoln and the GN Lincolnshire Coast line from Peterborough to Grimsby.

This then is a pictorial survey concentrated on a comparatively unconcentrated area. Although I was born and bred in Birmingham I have lived and worked here for nearly 50 years (war service excepted), and during the 1950s, when most of these pictures were taken, I was living in Stamford, a picturesque grey stone market town on one of the cross-country routes. Stamford's only passenger services 30 years ago, apart from being at the end of the short branch services from Seaton and Essendine, were Leicester-Peterborough trains stopping at all stations. The sight of an express headlamp code was a rarity until the closing of the M&GN in February 1959, after which eastbound summer weekend specials started to come through.

As a fairly junior bank clerk in the late 1940s and early 1950s my spare time was limited: only two weeks annual holiday, which was spent taking the family away, and no Saturday mornings off. Most of the interesting freight and ironstone workings took place between Monday and Friday, as did the whole range of the 1948 locomotive exchanges, on the East Coast main line, which passed within five miles of my doorstep and which I never saw. Bank managers would not have taken kindly to a request from their staff for time off to go and watch trains! In fact in the rural East Midlands railway photographers were few and far between and were regarded as distinctly eccentric by the general public, but not, fortunately for me, by a sympathetic Stamford stationmaster.

This is an area of rolling countryside bounded on the east by the highly fertile flatlands of the Fens and the Lincolnshire Marshes. It is dotted with market towns and has few industrial centres. To carry agricultural produce out and coal in were the main reasons why the network of railway lines were built, with passenger traffic as a secondary consideration – except where the seaside resorts of Mablethorpe, Skegness and the Norfolk coast were concerned. However, there is a limestone ridge which starts east of Bristol and runs in a great crescent northeastward through the counties of Gloucester, Oxford, Northampton, Rutland and Lincoln, ending some miles to the north of the City of Lincoln, whose magnificent cathedral stands so commandingly on the edge of this ridge, known there as the Lincoln Edge. Because of the ridge we have the beautiful creamy grey Cotswold towns and villages, and in Rutland and Lincolnshire the limestone was quarried for such buildings as Ely Cathedral and the House of Commons. In Northamptonshire it has a rusty colour which means iron ore, because of which Corby grew from a small village to a town with a mighty steelworks; the countryside around was torn up by huge excavators into a lunar landscape and the whole area for miles around was dotted with quarries and networks of industrial lines worked by a fascinating collection of little steam engines. To which until it was too late, I paid far too little attention. This gave rise to a different form of freight traffic loaded with ore to the foundries and returning empty for more. The quarries are closed now and the traces of the little lines that served them are slowly disappearing. While Corby is becoming a town of light industries in place of the blastfurnaces which used to light up the night sky. Coal traffic from South Yorkshire and other freight used to come southward through Lincoln on to the GN/GE joint line through Spalding to the Whitemoor marshalling yards at March for sorting, and the Lincolnshire coast main line carried the fast fish trains from Grimsby to the south, leaving behind them their distinctive aroma.

The north-south main lines with which this book is concerned carried express passenger services, all of which have now ceased. The Midland line was the route for trains to and from St Pancras to the North via Nottingham, the GN carried expresses from King's Cross to Grimsby and Cleethorpes, while the GN/GE joint line was part of the cross-country route for trains from Harwich to Liverpool via March, Spalding and Lincoln with portions for York and the northeast.

Road traffic was starting to take its toll of the vital freight traffic before World War 2 but it was in the 20 years after it that the slaughter of the railways was carried out. The sugar beet crop which used to be loaded into wagons in country station sidings now stands in heaps on the roadside awaiting the lorries to take it to the factory; and of the eight cross-country routes taking local passengers and – in summer time – holidaymakers to the seaside resorts, only two remain. One can still travel via Nottingham through Sleaford and Boston to Skegness, and the Midland line from Leicester to Peterborough has changed in character and gained in importance at the expense of the M&GN after the closure of which summer traffic for the holiday resorts on the Norfolk coast from the Midlands used this route in addition to the existing stopping passenger trains. Now only three out of the original 17 intermediate stations on the line remain open but there is a regular express service from Birmingham New Street, via Leicester and Peterborough to Norwich and Cambridge, as well as Leicester-Peterborough semi-fasts.

For the railway enthusiast in the last decade of steam there was a surprisingly rich variety of motive power to be seen on the cross-country routes, particularly of pre-grouping passenger engines; GN, GE and Midland on the M&GN, Midland and GC between Nottingham and Lincoln and, to start with, MR Class 2 and 3 4-4-0s and Compounds on the Leicester-Peterborough. However, in the mid-1950s administration of the eastern section of this latter line was transferred to the Eastern Region and responsibility for passenger service was shared between Leicester and March. Locomotives from March were also to be seen on through freight workings, and as the older types were extinguished more modern LMS and LNER engines appeared to be followed in turn by BR designs from Class 2 2-6-2 tanks to 'Britannias'. The one common factor was the LMS Ivatt Class 4 2-6-0 which could appear on any working right up to the end of steam.

The Seaton-Stamford and Seaton-Uppingham push-pull passenger services could produce some surprises. Rugby was the shed responsible for providing the motive power, which was housed in a little wooden sub shed situated in the angle of the junction at Seaton, of the Rugby-Peterborough line and the two branches to Uppingham and to Stamford via Luffenham Junction on the Leicester-Peterborough. In 1950 the duty was taken in turn by two MR class 1P 0-4-4 tanks, Nos 1420 and 1421, later Nos 58082/58083 in BR numbering. Occasionally both were out of action and then a LNWR Webb 2-4-2 tank

would appear, borrowed from the Leamington service. All these were replaced by Ivatt Class 2 2-6-2 tanks of both LMS and BR lineage. There was however one working for which Rugby was not responsible and this was the midday service from Seaton to Uppingham which on return to Seaton became the 2.30pm to Stamford. The engine was provided by Peterborough (Spital Bridge) and it found its way to duty by double-heading a westbound freight from home and detaching itself at Seaton. On completion of its duty at Stamford it left its one coach train and returned home light engine. It was this working which produced the LTS 4-4-2T, which became something of a tourist attraction, as well as GN Class C12 4-4-2Ts and LMS 'Jinty' tanks. Unlike the other turns this was not a push-pull operation.

The Bourne-Essendine branch, which until March 1957 used the GN terminus station at Stamford (East) alongside the River Welland, was the exclusive preserve of GN Class C12 4-4-2Ts until they were replaced by MS&L(GC) Class N5 0-6-2Ts during the final nine months of the branch's existence when the East station had been closed and trains ran into Stamford (Town). It offered a fascinating microcosm of the final days of the 'C12s' of which two were required to work the branch services, one for passenger and one for freight supplied by Peterborough (New England) and housed during their tour of duty in the small two engine sub shed at Stamford. The replacement for one of them would arrive at Essendine about 1pm each Saturday to take up its two weeks stay on the branch, while the replaced engine would return to Peterborough light, bunker first, on the up fast main line. On return to New England they were supposed to have a boiler washout but I have heard the branch driver complain that they were used for carriage shunting instead so that, on their return to Stamford, he and his mate had to do this chore themselves on a Sunday when there were no services.

From the number that I saw between 1948 and 1958 it would appear that the Stamford-Essendine was their final duty. Some would appear for two or three years, others I saw only once. In 1950 New England had six of them and as this supply wore out they were replaced by locomotives drawn from Louth, Boston, Grantham, Lincoln and sheds as far apart as Hornsey and Heaton, but from Stamford they had only one further destination – Doncaster! By mid-1958, after the closure of Stamford (East), the supply had run out and the last survivor on the branch, No 67398, had an ex-MS&L Class N5 0-6-2T as a companion. By September No 67398 had, ominously, been polished up and a month later she had gone, to be replaced by another 'N5'. Nine months later the whole branch closed.

Oddly enough the very last 'C12' to survive was also a Peterborough engine and also visited Stamford, but this, No 67352, was shedded at Spital Bridge and she found her way to Stamford via Seaton and the afternoon Seaton-Stamford service. She lasted until January 1959.

The Bourne-Essendine branch closed much earlier, in June 1951. Its motive power was also supplied by New England and consisted of GN Class J1 or J6 0-6-0s until supplanted by Ivatt Class 4 2-6-0s. The usual coaching stock was an ancient GN flat-roofed open saloon articulated pair. I rode in it once and was surprised at the smooth ride – earlier memories of GN flat roofed six-wheelers had led me to expect otherwise! Now, while Stamford enjoys a quite reasonable cross country semi-fast service, Bourne's railways are but a memory. From being a railway crossroads on the busy main line of the M&GN with branches to Sleaford and Essendine it is now hard to realise that there was a railway here at all. The station house, the unique Tudor mansion, still stands of course but is hardly recognisable as having had anything to do with trains, the track beds have been built on, but the goods shed still stands in solitary splendour, occupied by an old established firm of seed merchants who, in days gone by, relied on the railway for transport. The only crossing box to remain has been rebuilt as a private house, while out across the flat expanse of the fens to the east an odd isolated girder bridge over a river or dyke and a few gate keepers cottages show where once 11-coach expresses used to carry their loads of holidaymakers to and from the Norfolk coast.

The reader cannot have failed to notice the prominence given to Stamford and its environs in this introduction and this is for the simple reason that I lived there and my scope of action was rather limited as explained earlier. It is the area which I know most about and can talk about. To those whose interests are elsewhere in the East Midlands my apologies, but there wasn't much I could do about it. Besides Peterborough, which has been well documented by others, there was one other place of interest which I could reach fairly easily and that was Spalding. Spalding was well endowed with good vantage points for the observer and the photographer in the form of long iron footbridges spanning all the tracks and from which nothing could escape notice except traffic on the M&GN avoiding line to the south of the station and junctions. In any case this line suffered embankment subsidence in the mid-1950s and I never saw much using it.

As can be seen on the map, Spalding was the crossing place of three main lines. The first on the scene was the Peterborough-Grimsby line which, as far as Boston, formed part of the original Great Northern route to York, followed in the early 1860s by the bits and pieces to east and west which were later to form the M&GN and then by the GN/GE joint line from Whitemoor marshalling yards at March to Lincoln, which gave the GE access to South Yorkshire coal. There was a small two road shed of M&GN origin but which in the 1950s housed a variety of pre-grouping engines, mainly GN 0-6-0s outposted from New

England. All three routes converged to run through Spalding station; with a convenient overbridge at each end. Passenger traffic on all three routes was a mixture of stopping trains and expresses with Grimsby-King's Cross services on the GN and cross-country Harwich-Liverpool and Yarmouth-York trains on the March-Lincoln route. The M&GN had its famous 'Leicester' which was in fact a Yarmouth-Birmingham train – after the embankment trouble this and the heavy summer holiday traffic to the Norfolk coast ceased using the avoiding line and ran into the station where they reversed and changed engines. There was freight traffic on all routes although the M&GN traffic in flowers, fruit and vegetables had much fallen away to the roads, but that on the joint line to March it was substantial and produced some interesting motive power running through from York, including ex NE 'B16' 4-6-0s in original and both rebuilt forms. Many of the passenger train engines on this joint line were Doncaster-based, whilst Immingham 'B1s' and, later, 'Britannias' looked after the workings to King's Cross, and on the M&GN a wide variety of pre-grouping classes gave way to a rather monotonous diet of Ivatt Class 4 2-6-0s. Spalding is now a ghost station – gone are all routes except the GN from Peterborough leading onto the Joint onward to Lincoln, which serves as a relief route when the East Coast mainline is under repair. The only passenger service is an occasional DMU to and from Peterborough.

When I look at the equipment, and the financial aids, available to the photographer today I am at first inclined to be a bit envious and then to have second thoughts. So much sophisticated assistance is built into modern cameras that I wonder if perhaps the feeling of satisfaction in achieving success at a difficult subject with simple equipment is not being lost. Colour has also supplanted black and white to a large extent and in most cases the processing of this is done commercially.

Like many another chap of my day – I am talking about 55 years ago – my interest started at the age of 12 with a birthday present of a Kodak Box Brownie, and it took me about a year from then to realise that if I pointed it at a steam engine, held it steady and had the sun behind me, I might with luck make my own railway picture. If I remember rightly a GW Bulldog 4-4-0 called *Peacock* standing in the down bay at Snow Hill station Birmingham in 1929 was my first sitter. The film size was $2\frac{3}{4}$ x $3\frac{3}{4}$ orthochromatic of about 25 ASA, and the camera was no more than a square box with a single speed, about 1/25th sec, spring loaded shutter, a single glass fixed focus lens and the standard viewfinder of the day, a piece of ground glass about $\frac{1}{2}$in by $\frac{3}{4}$in beneath which was a mirror angled at 45°. Anyone who has ever tried to take a moving object with such a finder will know how difficult it was. That camera did however have two further facilities, one was the ability to hold the shutter open and the other was a strip of metal behind the lens which could be pulled out and had three holes of decreasing sizes punched in it. I had no text books on photography then but it did not take too long – with the aid of the ability to take time exposures and to stop down, as well as the very shape of the camera, which rested firmly on platform barrows, etc – to learn some very useful basic principles. I believe the Box Brownie cost 12/6d (62½p). About seven years later I acquired a folding Brownie which lacked the brief time and stop adjuster and which I found so useless that in about 1939 I managed to scrape together about £1.50 to buy a folding Kodak 620 with an F11 lens stopping down to F22 and shutter speeds up to 1/100th sec. This served me until 1947 when an unfortunate episode with a bath of hypo ruined it and I had to look round for replacement.

The camera which I found was a second-hand Zeiss Ikonta for £18. It had a range of shutter speeds up to 1/400th second and a Tessar 4.5 lens stopping down to f22. It also had an Albada sports type eye-level viewfinder, and at last I had an instrument capable of capturing fast moving subjects and those in dull light. Until then I had been concerned only with obtaining record shots of as many different classes of locomotive as possible. With the realisation of just what I could now tackle came the ambition to try and emulate the work of the men whose work was regularly featured in railway literature and it was to Ian Allan Ltd that I wrote for guidance – I got it in the form of a letter from the late O.J. Morris, which I still have. In essence the advice was that if I wanted to get the best from my negatives I must develop and print them myself, so I bought a couple of glass measures, a Gnome enlarger, pinched a couple of pudding basins from the kitchen, and set to work – success came when my first picture was published in *Trains Illustrated* of February 1950. Most of the pictures in this album were taken with that old Ikonta but its shutter gave out in 1960 and the decision was taken to 'go 35mm', inspired by the performance of a little Agfa Silette, which I used for colour, and the thought of how nice it would be to be able to go on a shed bash with a full 36 exposures loaded in the camera.

First of all I tried an Ambi-Silette with a 2.8 lens and 1/500 second shutter. It was a nice instrument but somehow I got too many unexplainable disappointments – in retrospect I think the shutter release may have been a bit rough. Anyway, in 1961 I went the whole hog with a Zeiss Pentacon, with focal plane shutter up to 1/1,000 second, fully interchangeable

lenses, the one fitted being a Zeiss Biotar f2. The Pentacon shutter gave out about 15 years ago but I still use that lens. The Pentacon was of course a single lens reflex of an early design, the mirror did not return after shooting until the shutter was re-cocked – a bit disconcerting at first but soon got used to. I now use a Practika with a range of lenses from 35mm to 400mm. But I have yet to own a camera with a built-in meter, preferring to use a well tried Weston selenium cell meter for those occasions when the eye might be unreliable. For those who still just point their automatic camera, snap and take the film to be commercially processed I would say you are missing a lot of photographic fun and not getting the best from your negatives. If to the pleasure of taking the picture you can add the expectancy with which you examine your film when you pull it out of the developing tank, and finally the fun of composing your picture in the enlarger and seeing it come to life in the developing dish, I think there is only one further pleasure the hobby can add – that of having others like and possibly admire what you have done. I am talking mainly about black and white film but, of recent years processes have become available for producing colour prints direct from transparencies and developing and printing colour print film at home.

I long ago discovered that if the final result did not please me it would not please anyone else although the reverse is not necessarily true. Apart from the urge to capture for oneself on film the sight and the atmosphere of the many facets of our railways, in my case the steam locomotive in particular, there comes the urge to please others with what you have made. I am not sure which has given me the greater pleasure, recreating on paper what I actually saw, the sight of one of my pictures reproduced in print, or the 'Thank you' letter from some driver, fireman, signalman or other railwayman to whom I have given a print. One wish cannot now be satisfied and that is to inspire others, as I was inspired, to go out and do what you have done or do it better. Unfortunately the subjects are no longer with us except in very limited form. Gone are the days when one could chat to a signalman in a lonely box and wait for the block bells and clash of the semaphore signal coming off to herald a distant plume of steam and the coming of who knew what until it was squarely in the viewfinder.

P. H. Wells
Bourne

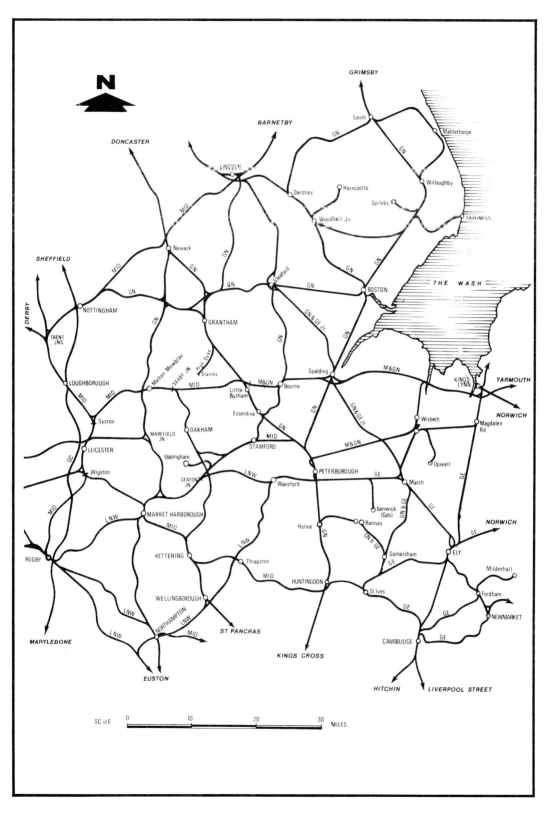

N

GRIMSBY

BARNETBY

DONCASTER

Louth

Mablethorpe

LINCOLN

GN

GN

Bardney

Horncastle

Willoughby

GN

Spilsby

SKEGNESS

Woodhall Jn

SHEFFIELD

Newark

MID

GN

GN

Sleaford

GN

BOSTON

THE WASH

DERBY

NOTTINGHAM

GN

GN

GRANTHAM

GN

GN&GE Jt

GN

TRENT
JNS.

GN

Melton Mowbray

High Dyke

Stainby

Spalding

M&GN

KING'S
LYNN

YARMOUTH

LOUGHBOROUGH

MID

MID

SAXBY JN

MID

M&GN

Bourne

GN

GN&GE Jt

Wisbech

Magdalen
Rd.

NORWICH

Little
Bytham

Syston

Essendine

MID

Upwell

MAREFIELD
JN

OAKHAM

GN

M&GN

GE

LEICESTER

STAMFORD

GE

Wigston

Uppingham

PETERBOROUGH

GE

March

NORWICH

MID

SEATON
JN

LNW

Wansford

Benwick
(Gds)

GN & GE

GE

GE

Holme

Ramsey

MARKET HARBOROUGH

MID

GN

GN & GE

Somersham

ELY

RUGBY

KETTERING

LNW

Thrapston

GE

Mildenhall

MID

HUNTINGDON

GE

Fordham

WELLINGBOROUGH

St Ives

GE

NEWMARKET

LNW

NORTHAMPTON

LNW

MID

ST PANCRAS

GE

LNW

CAMBRIDGE

GE

MARYLEBONE

EUSTON

KINGS CROSS

HITCHIN

LIVERPOOL STREET

SCALE   0   10   20   30   MILES

9

Above:
BR Standard Class 5 No 73070 of Bletchley runs through Castle station with an up through freight on 2 May 1964.

Left:
BR Standard Class 4 No 75013 of Bletchley runs in from the Roade direction with a down freight on 2 May 1964. The Peterborough and Bedford lines go off to the left.

Below left:
Ex LNW Class G2 No 9437 of Edge Hill comes through Castle station with an up through freight on 28 April 1951.

Above right:
Ex GE Class D16/3 4-4-0 No 62599 of Peterborough (Spital Bridge) in the down bay at Castle station with a Market Harborough train on 2 April 1955.

Right:
On the last day of the service to Peterborough LMS Class 5 No 45113 carrying a Camden shedplate stands in the south bay with the last return working on 2 May 1964. On the right is LMS Ivatt Class 2 2-6-2T No 41225 of Wellingborough on a Bedford train.

Top:
No 45113 on the last train running into Oundle on 2 May 1964.

Left:
No 45113 runs into Wellingborough LNW station on the last run back to Peterborough on 2 May 1964.

Above:
LMS Class 5 4-6-0s Nos 44667 and 45342 of Derby pause at Wellingborough Midland station with a brake test special fitted freight from Toton to Brent on 24 January 1951.

Above:
Oundle station buildings from the forecourt on 3 October 1960. One of the many in the area constructed in grey limestone.

Below:
LMS Class 4 0-6-0 No 44524 of Northampton pauses at Oundle with a westbound local freight on 3 October 1960.

Above right:
Nassington Quarries near Wansford. The entire motive power stock consisting of 0-6-0STs *Ring Haw* and *Jacks Green* take a weekend rest outside their shed on 25 June 1970. Both have been preserved.

Right:
The shed layout at Nassington Quarries photographed from the headshunt in July 1970. The 'main line' swings off to the right past the single storey offices.

Above:
Just to the west of Yarwell Tunnel is the junction where the Rugby-Peterborough line joins in. LMS Class 4F 0-6-0 No 44509 of March comes out of the eastern end of this short tunnel into Wansford with a loaded ore train from Nassington Quarries on 4 October 1960.

Right:
LMS Fowler Class 4 2-6-4T No 42353 of Northampton runs through Wansford station, now bereft of its up platform, with a Peterborough-Northampton train on 4 October 1960.

Right:
LMS Class 5 No 44806 of Nottingham accelerates southward out of Kettering with an up cup-tie special on 18 March 1963.

Below:
LMS 'Jubilee' class 4-6-0s Nos 45560 *Prince Edward Island* of Nottingham and 45614 *Leeward Islands* of Kentish Town double-head a St Pancras bound express into Kettering station on 17 August 1957. This train has come via Melton Mowbray and Oakham, joining the Midland main at Glendon South Junction.

Left:
Shrouded in leaking steam LMS Compound 4-4-0 No 41050 of Kentish Town gets under way with a down main line stopping train for Leicester on 16 November 1952.

Below left:
Ex MR Class 2P 4-4-0 No 40461 of Nottingham leaves with a down stopping train bound for the Nottingham loop on 17 August 1957.

Below:
Normally one would not expect to find an SR Class W 2 6 4T in Kettering shed yards. Sadly the reason for No 31922's presence is that she is due for a nearby scrapyard. The date 22 March 1964.

Right:
Ex MR Class 1F 0-6-0T No 1889 in the shed yard on 24 April 1948. The coal wagon is on the coaling stage ramp and a Midland Johnson Class 3 0-6-0 stands behind.

Below right:
Another view of the same spot nine years later. LMS Ivatt Class 2 2-6-0 No 46403 of Kettering is on the ramp while Stanier Class 8F 2-8-0 No 48142 of Coalville stands by the water column on 17 August 1957.

Above:
A pre-war scene at Cambridge shed with ex MR Class 2 0-6-0 No 3195 standing outside having been serviced preparatory to taking a return working to Kettering. Taken in the summer of 1939.

Below:
LMS Ivatt Class 2 2-6-0 No 46403 of Kettering in the down bay at Cambridge with a Kettering train on 23 April 1958. Alongside is ex GE Class B12/3 4-6-0 No 61516 of Cambridge with a stopping train for Kings Lynn.

Cambridge

Above:
'Britannia' Pacific No 70039 *Sir Christopher Wren* of Stratford brings a down express up to the crossover to gain access to the north end on 23 April 1958.

Below:
Ex GE Class E4 2-4-0 No 62785 takes water at the north end of the through platform on 23 April 1958.

Top:
No 62785 stands in the north bay at Cambridge with a Mildenhall train on 23 April 1958. She was the sole survivor of her class at this time and finished her time on this branch before being withdrawn for preservation.

Above:
Fordham Junction at 8am on 1 May 1958. No 62785 swings away towards Exton Road Halt and Barnwell Junction with a Mildenhall-Cambridge train whilst an Ely train hauled by Class N7/4 0-6-2T No 69616 stands in the platform.

Above:
GE 'Super Claud' Class D16/2 No 8792 piloting ex GC Class D9 4-4-0 No 2603 bring a prewar Kings Lynn-Liverpool Street express into the station. A 1938 scene No 8792 was renumbered 2519.

Below:
Ex GE Class D15 4-4-0 No 8830 (later 2561) rests quietly in the sidings in 1938.

Above:
'Britannia' Pacific No 70031 *Byron* of Longsight passing Glendon (South) Junction with a Manchester/St Pancras express on 19 April 1961. The Nottingham line diverges to the right behind the second coach.

Below:
LMS Class 5 No 44861 of Nottingham joins the main line at Glendon South Junction with an up stopping train on 19 April 1961.

Left:
LMS Class 8F 2-8-0 No 48380 of Kettering arrives at Corby steelworks sidings with an up empty freight on 16 March 1963.

Below:
A Stewarts & Lloyds 0-6-0ST comes away from the furnaces with hoppers full of molten slag and a very necessary match wagon on 4 June 1964.

Right:
Stewarts & Lloyds No 9 shunts a rake of hoppers towards the furnaces on 18 March 1963.

Left:
Stanier '8F' 2-8-0 No 48759 of Kettering bursts out of Glaston Tunnel (1,642yd) with a down freight on 14 August 1954.

Below:
The short level stretch with freight lay-byes between Glaston and Wing Tunnels gives 'Jubilee' No 45579 *Punjab* of Kentish Town an opportunity to pick up speed with a down Nottingham & Bradford express on 20 September 1956.

Right:
'Jubilee' No 45619 *Nigeria* of Leeds comes out of Manton Tunnel and takes the right fork at the junction with an up express on 27 March 1954. The Peterborough line via Stamford veers away eastward.

Below right:
Class J39 0-6-0 No 64896 of Peterborough (Spital Bridge) takes the old Syston and Peterborough route at Manton Junction with an eastbound freight on 27 March 1954.

Above:
'Jubilee' 4-6-0 No 45565 *Victoria* of Leeds Holbeck tackles the bank from Manton Tunnel to Oakham with a down express on a very wet afternoon on 7 August 1954.

Below:
Oakham station with a grubby Ivatt Class 4 2-6-0 No 43081 of Peterborough New England and a short down stopper on 6 August 1960.

Above right:
Class 4F 0-6-0 No 44477 of Sheffield Grimethorpe roars through Oakham station with a return summer Saturday special from the East Coast via Peterborough East and North on 6 August 1960.

Right:
Oakham's up starter and level crossing box on 6 August 1960. The road is the mainroad to Nottingham and there will doubtless be quite a string of traffic waiting for the Stanier Class 8F 2-8-0 to rumble across with a southbound breakdown train.

Left:
The 1964 'East Midlander' bound for Banbury,
Didcot, Newbury to Eastleigh and back via
Salisbury and Swindon pauses at Rugby Central
for water behind 'Duchess' Pacific No 46251 *City
of Nottingham* of Crewe North on 9 May 1964.
The 'Duchess' came off at Didcot and took over
the return working at Swindon. Within six
months only her nameplates survived.

Below left:
BR Standard Class 5 4-6-0 No 73157 of Woodford
Halse gets away smartly from the Central station
on 17 October 1964 with the afternoon
Marylebone-Nottingham.

Top right:
BR Standard Class 9 2-10-0 No 92030 of
Kirby-in-Ashfield rumbles across the girder
bridge carrying the GC main line over the LNW
West Coast main line with an up freight on 17
October 1964.

Above right:
The scene just south of Rugby Midland station at
the flyover junctions with the Northampton and
Market Harborough lines on 27 October 1963. The
cause of the mess was the need to lower the
trackbed of the West Coast main line to
accommodate overhead electric wires. The line in
the foreground is the down main and in the
background can be seen the girder bridge
carrying the GC main line.

Right:
Stanier Class 4 2-6-4T No 42446 of Rugby stands
in the down bay of Rugby Midland's island
platform with a Leicester train on 7 September
1957.

Above:
'Britannia' Pacific No 70014 *Iron Duke* of Trafford Park departs on the Midland main line on 7 September 1958 with a down express. The LNW Rugby-Peterborough platforms and lines are on the right as is the sub-shed to Rugby just out of the picture on the right.

Right:
LMS Ivatt Class 2 2-6-0 No 6401 leaves with an up MR main line stopping train in 1948. This class was not introduced until 1946 and pictures of them in LMS livery are comparatively rare. Photographed from the LNW platform.

Below right:
The coaling stage at Market Harborough with LNW Class G2 0-8-0 No 49435 of Rugby on 13 October 1956.

Left:
Hughes 'Crab' 2-6-0 No 42799 of Saltley runs light on the up line through Ashton & Weston station on 3 July 1949.

Below:
Ex GC Class 04/8 2-8-0 No 63791 of March leaves Welham Junction on the Peterborough line with a down through freight on 18 May 1963. Behind the engine's cab in the background are Welham sidings and the LNW/GN Joint line to Melton Mowbray and Nottingham can be seen swinging away to the right.

Above:
GN Class C12 4-4-2T No 67352 of Peterborough (Spital Bridge) stands on the down main line at Seaton to take a drink, presumably because the pipe will not reach the Stamford/Uppingham branches bay line in the background. She has arrived here from her home shed double-heading an up freight and, after a turn on the Uppingham branch, will take the one-coach branch train to Stamford whence she will return home light engine. The date is 18 September 1956 and this engine is one of the few still retaining the original bunker without the flared top extension. She proved to be the last survivor of the class.

Above left:
LMS Fairburn Class 4 2-6-4T No 42062 of Rugby bustles away from Seaton with a Peterborough train on 19 September 1956. Just visible in the left background is the northern end of Harringworth viaduct carrying the Midland main line to Nottingham and under which this train has passed via the bridge seen behind the train.

Left:
Kings Cliffe station on 13 January 1962 with Class 5 4-6-0 No 44760 of Rugby departing on a Peterborough train while a Birmingham bound DMU appears on the right.

Peterborough

Above:
The Great Eastern's East station on a bitterly cold day during the big freeze of the 1962/3 winter. This shot taken with a 135mm telephoto lens on 19 January 1963 shows LMS Class 5 4-6-0 No 44674 of Leicester waiting to depart with a Leicester stopping train via Stamford, Oakham and Melton. The GE arrival and departure line with two platform faces is on the left.

Below:
Class 5 4-6-0 No 45113 about to depart for Northampton on 2 May 1964, the last day of the working. The shape of things to come in the form of BR Bo-Bo Type 2 No D5023 of Ipswich stands on the right.

Above:
GE Class D16/3 4-4-0 No 62588 of March runs in under the East station signalbox from Peterborough North with an eastbound express on 26 February 1954. This engine was one of the five 'Clauds' rebuilt with 8in piston valves.

Left:
'Footballer' Class B17/4 4-6-0 No 61651 *Derby County* of Colchester has just arrived with a down fast at the East station's double-platform line on 10 April 1954.

Above right:
A westbound troop special hauled by 'B1' Class 4-6-0 No 61113 of Cambridge heads out of the East station on 10 April 1954 and takes the righthand fork of the junction under the East Coast main line which will bring the train into Peterborough North and thence possibly up to Catterick Camp. The left hand line is the ex LNW one to Rugby and Northampton.

Right:
Class A4 Pacific No 60022 *Mallard* of King's Cross with a down express approaching Peterborough North on the East Coast main line on 11 July 1955.

Left:
The south end of the North station with 'B1' No 61391 of New England waiting to depart with a society special to various little used freight lines to the east on 9 September 1956. This train was an amalgamation of two, one from King's Cross and one from Nottingham.

Below:
A picture of GN Class C1 Atlantic No 4403 taken with a Box Brownie camera about 50 years ago. She is acting as stand-by in the down bay at Peterborough North.

Right:
This is not an unusual double-heading! Class A1 Pacific No 60116 *Hal o' the Wind* of Heaton is about to take over a down express from the 'A4' Pacific seen departing on the left towards New England. Ivatt Class 4 2-6-0 No 43090 of Kings Lynn and will depart over the M&GN via Sutton Bridge when the road is clear. The date is 9 April 1951.

Below right:
Class A3 Pacific No 60039 *Sandwich* of King's Cross gets away smartly on the main line with a down Newcastle express on 31 January 1959. The M&GN tracks are in the immediate foreground whilst the MR to Leicester are just beyond the appropriate signal.

Above:
MR Class 2 4-4-0 No 40452 of Leicester casts a smokescreen across her train as she gets away with a Peterborough-Leicester stopper on 31 January 1959 in the immediate foreground are the M&GN tracks beyond the East Coast main line and New England yards behind the train.

Below:
Ivatt Class 4 2-6-0 No 43107 of South Lynn takes the M&GN road out of Peterborough with an eastbound passenger train on 14 February 1959.

Above:
GE Class J17 0-6-0 No 65562 of March takes some truckloads of enthusiasts out of Benwick on the freight only branch returning to Three Horseshoes Junction on the Peterborough March line on 9 September 1956.

Below:
Complete with express indicators and headboard No 65562 stands with her now deserted train as the passengers make their way back to more comfortable accommodation in the main line train at Whittlesey on 9 September 1956.

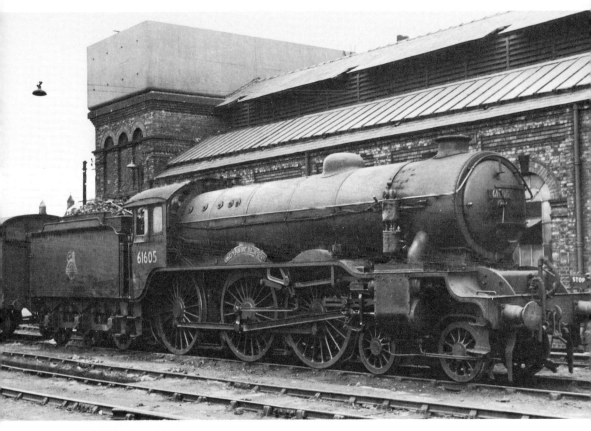

Above:
Class B17/6 No 61605 *Lincolnshire Regiment* at its home shed at March on 27 July 1952.

Left:
One-time Royal engine Class D16/3 4-4-0 No 62618 of Cambridge, still maintained in green livery and polished metalwork stops at Wisbech East with a Kings Lynn-Cambridge train on 27 July 1952.

Above right:
The fireman of Class D16/3 No 62548 of March prepares to take the tablet from the Wisbech East signalman for the single line section to Mahdalen Road junction on the Ely-Kings Lynn line. The train is a summer weekend special from the Midlands to Hunstanton via Peterborough and the date 27 July 1952.

Right:
Wisbech shed on 27 July 1952. Yard shunter Class J69 0-6-0T No 68664 from Kings Lynn stands outside whilst inside are two Class J70 0-6-0 Tram engines Nos 68223 and 68225 for use on the Wisbech and Upwell tramway.

Left:
Ivatt Class 2 2-6-2T No 41278 of Rugby leaves Seaton junction on the Uppingham line on 15 September 1956. The line on the left is to Stamford via Luffenham junction on the MR Leicester-Peterborough line whilst the Rugby-Peterborough line is out of sight behind the bank on the left and the Harringworth viaduct of the MR Nottingham line seen stretching away towards Corby and Kettering.

Below:
Ivatt Class 2 No 41279 is a Kettering engine and must have been borrowed for use on the branch. She is seen here on 12 March 1960 passing under a road bridge about a mile from the terminus.

Right:
Another of the same class No 41214 stands in Uppingham station after arrival from Seaton on 18 August 1956. She is a Rugby engine.

Below right:
A rare and unexpected catch. With the Stamford line in the foreground MR Class 2 4-4-0 No 40418 of Burton swings in from Uppingham with an inspection saloon on 23 September 1954

Right:
Class C12 4-4-2T No 67352 of Spital Bridge runs through the cutting at South Luffenham with a one-coach Seaton-Stamford train on 19 September 1956. She will shortly join the Leicester-Peterborough line at Luffenham Junction.

Below:
Luffenham Junction on 29 March 1958. LTS 4-4-2T No 41975 of Spital Bridge comes off the Seaton line with the afternoon train for Stamford.

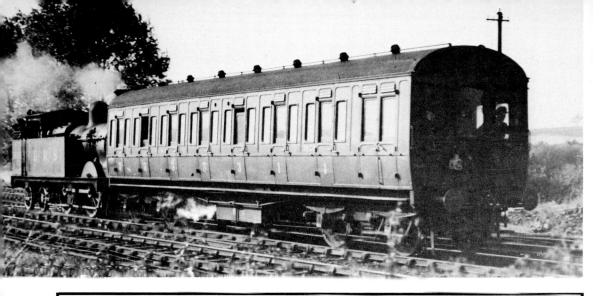

Above:
The driver can be seen in his compartment as the mid-day Seaton-Stamford auto train approaches the end of its journey, propelled by MR Class 1P 0-4-4T on 23 October 1948. The engine is one of a pair of consecutively numbered locos, LMS No 1420/1 later BR No 58082/3 from Rugby and sub-shedded at Seaton, which maintained the branch services at this time. This is No 58082.

Below:
Occasionally both MR 0-4-4Ts were out of service and on 24 December 1949 Rugby provided LNW Class 1P 2-4-2T No 6683 seen here, patterned by long winter shadows, taking a drink at the end of Stamford down platform after arrival with the mid-day working from Seaton.

Below:
The westbound West-Bridge freight leaves Glenfield Tunnel behind MR Class 2 0-6-0 No 58148 of Coalville on 7 July 1962.

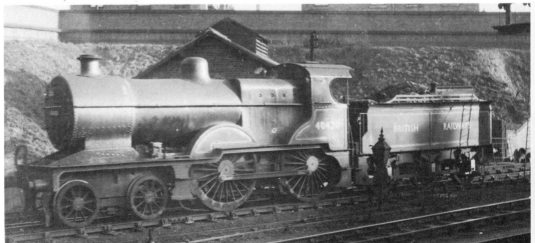

Left:
A Carlisle Kingmoor 'Crab' No 42883 leaves Leicester London Road on 19 November 1955 with a football special for Nottingham – presumably borrowed by Leicester shed for the occasion.

Below left:
MR Class 2 4-4-0 No 40420 comes off shed at Leicester London Road on 19 February 1949.

Above:
The south (up) bay at Leicester Central on 15 December 1955 with Class A3 Pacific No 60062 *Minoru* wearing a King's Cross shedplate and 'B1' 4-6-0 No 61188 of Colwick awaiting their next turn.

Below:
GC Class 04/3 No 63733 of Darlington approaches the north end of Leicester Central with an up through freight on 6 December 1955. This is an ex ROD engine fitted with steam brake only and no water pick-up scoop.

Above:
Belgrave Road station on 16 July 1961 with Class B1 4-6-0 No 61209 of Colwick making a vigorous departure with an 11-coach summer Saturdays only excursion to Skegness.

Right:
Arrival at Belgrave Road on 15 July 1962 with 'B1' No 61177 of Colwick bringing in a return working from Skegness.

Belgrave Road and the joint line to Melton

Below:
Class B1 No 61285 of Colwick emerges from Thurnby Tunnel with a return working from Skegness on 28 July 1962. This was a Sunday when there was only a Skegness working. On Saturdays there was also one to Mablethorpe.

Bottom:
The east end of the 516yd Thurnby Tunnel with 'B1' No 61142 of Colwick getting under way up the grade after a stop at Thurnby & Scraptoft station on 9 July 1961 with a Skegness train. The state of the track shows why there was a 25mph restriction as far as Marefield Junction where the GN branch joined the LNW/GN Joint.

Left and right:
On the Joint line south of Marefield 'Austerity' 2-8-0 No 90717 of Colwick brings a down freight out of the short tunnel near East Norton on 2 August 1962 and (*right*) passes through East Norton station. The cutting here has now been filled in and the earth brought up to road level.

Above:
After the closure of Belgrave Road the RCTS ran a special over the branch here seen passing the shell of Lowesby box on 18 May 1963 behind Black Five No 45238 of Nottingham.

Left:
Lonely Marefield Junction where the GN branch to Belgrave Road left the LNW/GN Joint line. On 2 September 1961 Class B1 No 61188 of Colwick takes the Leicester road with a return excursion from Skegness.

Below left:
On a very wet Sunday morning on 15 July 1962 Class B1 No 61177 of Colwick roars up the grade through John o' Gaunt station with a Belgrave Road-Skegness excursion.

Right:
Class B1 No 61092 of Colwick waits for the right away at Melton North with a return working from Mablethorpe to Belgrave Road on 23 June 1962.

Below:
'B1' No 61177 again. Here she is bringing a return working from Skegness into Melton North on a Saturday, 15 July 1962.

Above:
Ketton & Collyweston station with MR Class 2 No 40526 of Burton entering with a Peterborough-Leicester stopper on a wintry 26 February 1955.

Left:
Industrial line in the Welland Valley. Ketton Cement No 5 winds up the private line from the MR in the far background to the works with a van on 19 September 1956. This line is still used though steam has long gone.

Above right:
On 26 November 1961 through working to Peterborough had been interrupted and services to Leicester were starting at Stamford. In this view taken from the A1 by-pass overbridge Fowler Class 4 2-6-4T of Leicester sets out for home with a stopping train through the frozen Welland meadows and with the town of Stamford just visible in the background.

Right:
Bournville Compound 4-4-0 No 41156 leaves Stamford behind on her way to Peterborough with an eastbound stopper on 27 April 1954.

Above:
Helpston station with MR Class 2 4-4-0 No 40526 of Burton arriving with a Peterborough-Leicester stopper on 20 June 1953.

Right:
MR Class 2 4-4-0 No 40542 of Leicester passes Stamford's outer up distant with a stopping train for Leicester on 7 January 1950.

Above:
The terminus for the Seaton and Essendine branch services as well as being an intermediate town on the Leicester-Peterborough route of the one-time Syston & Peterborough Railway. In the mid-1950s control of this part of the line passed to the ER and March engines started to share the workings. Here on 4 April 1962 'Britannia' Pacific No 70003 *John Bunyan* of March restarts the 8.20am to Leicester.

Below:
Steam at Stamford in the heyday of the MR Class 2s. No 40559 of Peterborough Spital Bridge is shunting the yard while No 40543 of Leicester gets under way with the midday stopping train for Leicester on 23 February 1952.

Left:
MR Class 3 0-6-0 No 3319 of Mansfield drifts into Stamford (Town) with a Westbound freight in 1948.

Below:
Toton Garratt No 47979 opens up again after negotiating the reverse curves through the short tunnel and overbridges to the east of Stamford station. The date 17 January 1953.

Right:
One of the original 1912 batch of MR Class 4F 0-6-0s No 44020 of Leicester pounds through with an up freight on 20 December 1951. The Seaton branch departure bay is on the right.

Left:
'B1' class 4-6-0 No 61252 accelerates away from Stamford with a return summer Saturday working from the Norfolk coast to the Midlands. She was recorded in 1960 as a Cambridge engine but, having lost her shedplate I imagine she was a March engine on 17 August 1963 when this picture was taken.

Below left:
MR Class 4F 0-6-0 No 43988 of Leicester brings a down (eastbound) freight out of the short tunnel to the east of the Town station and past the yards of the East station on 30 April 1963. Until March 1957 Essendine branch trains used the East, a terminus station, but after its closure used a crossover, behind the photographer, to run into the Town station for the final two years of the branch service.

Above:
The East station after closure and removal of the canopy over the entrance. An engraved stone plaque over the central window carries the arms of the House of Exeter.

Below:
Stamford East station on 2 March 1957, the day it closed. GN Class C12 4-4-2T No 67376 of New England waits to depart with the 2.30pm for Essendine. The other platform face used to be used for trains to Wansford before that service was withdrawn over 50 years ago and on the right is the River Welland. The 'empties' on the bufferbeam indicate that No 67376 is due to return to her home shed after her two week's stint sub-shedded at Stamford. The exchange with the relief engine will take place at Essendine, whence she will proceed light engine on the up fast of the East Coast main line.

Top:
'C12' 4-4-2T No 67368 of New England brings the early morning transfer freight from the Town yards to the east yards over the crossover from the MR to the GN on 15 March 1952. The signals over the fourth van are at the end of the East station platform.

Above:
In June 1958 the exclusive reign of the 'C12' 4-4-2Ts was broken as the supply began to run out. The replacements were the even older ex MS&L Class N5 0-6-2Ts and here on 17 July 1958 No 69262 of that class takes the 7.30am Stamford (Town)-Essendine over the crossover onto the branch. The closed East station can be seen over the second coach.

Top:
Double-chimneyed Ivatt Class 4 2-6-0 No 43047 of Saltley bustles away from Stamford with a Leicester-Peterborough train on 6 September 1953. On the right are the Essendine branch lines and the East shed.

Above:
Stamford East shed on 13 April 1952 with Class C12 No 67357 of New England shunting wagons at the coaling stage. The shed could accommodate two of these engines during their staggered two-weekly tours of duty on the branch.

Above right:
A pair of hands apparently lifted in supplication appear out of the cab of New England C12 4-4-2T No 67398 as she climbs out of Stamford over the River Welland bridge on her way to Essendine on 27 September 1958. The days of the class are very nearly over and in fact this was the last one to operate on the branch, which might explain the 'prayers' from one of the crew!

Right:
'C12' No 67361 leaves Ryhall & Belmisthorpe, the only intermediate station with the 7.33am Stamford (East)-Essendine on 17 May 1950.

Below:
Early morning at Essendine on 26 June 1954. The East Coast main lines are in the foreground as Class C12 No 67357 comes off the branch and past the south box with the 7.33am from Stamford (East).

Essendine

Above:
Class J6 0-6-0 No 64228 runs into the Bourne branch bay with the Bourne-Essendine branch train consisting of a GN flat roofed articulated pair of open saloons on 14 October 1950. The branch can be seen curving sharply away eastward behind the water column. The fast East Coast main lines are in the foreground.

Right:
Class B1 No 61177 of Grantham brings the afternoon Grantham to Peterborough stopper into Essendine on 9 July 1949 with a rake of what must be M&GN coaching stock.

Below right:
Ex NER Class B16/1 No 1400 of Leeds Neville Hill comes past the South box and into the station with a down fitted freight on the fast line on 9 September 1948. I believe she did become BR No 61400 but had to be renumbered 61469 when her original number was required by new 'B1' construction. The Bourne branch set is on the left.

73

Above:
A 'B12/3' on main line duty. No 61554 of
Grantham brings a four-coach special in from
Grantham on 3 June 1951. At Essendine coaches
were added, six from Stamford and two from
Bourne, to make up a substantial school
excursion to the Festival of Britain which, I
believe, then ran non-stop to King's Cross.

Below:
After withdrawal from BR service Class A3 *Flying
Scotsman* was rebuilt at Doncaster to her prewar
condition before being handed over to private
ownership. Before being painted in LNER colours
the works tested her on a 14-coach empty train to
Peterborough and back on 7 February 1963. She
is seen here on the return trip in freezing
conditions just north of Essendine.

Bourne-Essendine

Above:
Ivatt Class 4 2-6-0 No 43082 of New England
pauses at Braceborough Spa with the afternoon
Bourne-Essendine train on 7 April 1951, two
months before closure. Braceborough's spa
never developed and the station was quite
isolated, the road thereto ending in farmland just
to the left of the crossing gates.

Right:
Class J6 No 4220 comes under the road bridge at
Carlby with a Bourne-Essendine train on 9 July
1949. A New England engine sub-shedded at
Spalding.

Left:
Not a usual sight on the East Coast main line in this area – ex GC Class A5 4-6-2T No 69808 of Grantham with a stopping train for Peterborough on 5 June 1957. It was on this stretch of line where the world speed record for steam traction was broken.

Below left:
BR Class 9 2-10-0 No 92192 of Doncaster approached the station with a down through freight on 28 February 1959. Above the left-hand support of the station footbridge can be seen the girder bridge carrying the M&GN Saxby to Bourne section on which this was the last day of operation. Today not only has this bridge gone but so has the station and there is nothing to be seen but a clear stretch of track.

Right:
On the long climb to Stoke summit Class A3 Pacific No 60105 *Victor Wild* of King's Cross roars through the station with a down express on 4 April 1951.

Below:
With the footplate crew taking it easy, ex-GC Class Q4/2 No 63240 of Grantham trundles an up freight down the bank towards Essendine on 14 July 1950.

Left:
Austerity 2-8-0 No 90003 of Peterborough Spital Bridge brings an eastbound freight towards the station on the Midland line on 7 April 1951. The junction for the M&GN trains is beyond the bracket signal on the left.

Below:
Ivatt Class 4 2-6-0 No 43082 of New England waits for the right away with a Spalding train on 7 April 1951. The Midland main line is behind the train and can just be seen through the arch of the bridge.

Above:
Class D3 4-4-0 No 2128 of New England eases off after the sharp climb from Little Bytham as she runs past the goods dock into Castle Bytham station with a Spalding-Nottingham train on 27 September 1949.

Above right:
Ivatt Class 4 2-6-0 No 43058 approaches Castle Bytham with the last through working to Nottingham on 28 February 1959. The length of the train, 11 coaches filled mainly with enthusiasts bidding farewell to the line, compared with the usual three, must have been an effort even for these sturdy machines.

Right:
High above the East Coast main line, itself on an embankment, at Little Bytham, Ivatt Class 4 2-6-0 No 43060 of New England brings the very last 'Leicester' across the girder bridge making for Spalding on 28 February 1959, where it was replaced by sister engine No 43093 for the final part of the journey to Yarmouth.

Top:
Ex GN Class D3 4-4-0 No 62131 of New England about to depart with the 4pm for Saxby and Nottingham on 8 October 1949. This engine was unique among GN Ivatt 4-4-0s in having separate driving wheel splashers.

Above:
GN Class J2 0-6-0 No 65017 of Boston stands outside Bourne shed on 8 October 1949. Having brought in a freight over the line from Sleaford she has been turned and awaits the return trip.

Top right:
Ivatt Class 4 2-6-0 No 43062 of New England stands, parked off the turntable beside the water tower at Bourne shed on 7 April 1951.

Right:
GE Class D16/3 No 62573 of South Lynn heads an express for Yarmouth out of Bourne on 8 October 1949.

Above:
Just north of the junction where the line to
Grimsby left the East Coast main line Class A1
Pacific No 60149 *Amadis* of Doncaster accelerates
over the main line water troughs with the down
'Aberdonian' on 15 July 1954. The time was
about 9.20pm and double summer time made
this shot possible.

Right:
Class J6 0-6-0 No 64232 of Doncaster gets under
way with a down freight on 15 July 1954 on the
down slow beside Werrington troughs, the
control tower for which can be seen just to the
left of the engine. The Grimsby line swings away
behind this tower, while the MR
Peterborough-Leicester trucks are on the right.

Below right:
Between Spalding and Peterborough Class B1
4-6-0 No 61143 of Immingham is about to cross
the A16 road at Deeping St Nicholas with a
Grimsby-Peterborough train on 12 September
1959.

Above:
Class B 16/2 4-6-0 No 61475 of York swings into Spalding on the GN/GE joint line having just passed under the through M&GN avoiding line with a down freight of empty flat wagons on 29 April 1958. This engine is one of the seven Gresley rebuilds of the 69 NER three cylinder engines of the class and has conjugated valve gear. They were very difficult to distinguish from the later Thompson rebuilds which had separate sets of valve gear, the only external difference being that the radius rods behind the outside valve spindles were bent to accommodate the linkage to the middle cylinder.

Right:
Class 01 2-8-0 No 63678 of March takes the GN/GE joint line with an up freight on 29 April 1958. She has just left the Peterborough line with the M&GN lines to Saxby on the far left. The eastbound M&GN line to Sutton Bridge and beyond swings sharply away under the end of the train and can just be seen through the shrubbery on the right. This class of Thompson rebuilds from GC class 04s were originally intended to be the standard heavy freight engines of the LNER.

Left:
Ivatt Class 4 2-6-0 No 43014 of York passes through the station with an up freight for the GN/GE Joint on 26 April 1958, bound for Whitemoor yards.

Below:
Spalding only had a small sub shed to New England and it came as a surprise to find 'B17/4' 4-6-0 No 61663 *Everton* of Stratford in ex-works condition standing dead in the yard on 16 February 1958. Something must have gone wrong on the journey home after a refit.

Right:
Class O2/3 2-8-0 No 63971 of Retford takes the freight avoiding line with a down freight on 12 October 1957.

Below right:
Class B1 4-6-0 No 61285 of Doncaster makes a vigorous get away with a stopping train for March on 12 October 1957.

Above left:
Class B16/1 4-6-0 No 61424 of York comes through the station on the up Joint line with a freight for Whitemoor yards on 4 March 1950. The right-hand platform line is the Grimsby-Pcterborough which had no connection with the joint line until they merged at the south end.

Left:
GE Class J19 0-6-0 No 64656 of March ambles through the station from the yards on the north side with a short pick-up freight for the joint line on 4 March 1950.

Above:
Doncaster 'B1' No 61247 gets away with a down joint line express on 12 September 1959.

Right:
Ivatt Class 4 2-6-0 No 43142 of South Lynn takes the M&GN line eastward out of Spalding with a stopping train on 7 June 1954. The GN & Joint lines are in the background with the westbound M&GN beyond.

Above right:
Ivatt Class 4 2-6-0 No 40060 of New England approaches the Ouse Bridge at South Lynn with a Yarmouth train on 15 August 1954.

Right:
South Lynn Shed on 27 July 1952. In the foreground is New England 'J6' No 64228 whilst other types to be seen are GE 0-6-0 Classes J17 and J19, GE 4-4-0 Class D16/3, GE 4-6-0 Class B12/3, GN 2-6-0 Class K2 and an Ivatt Class 4 2-6-0.

Below:
GE Class J17 0-6-0 No 65530 of Kings Lynn leaves her home yard with an up freight on 29 July 1959.

Top:
For a short while the ex-BSC shed at Market Overton in the heart of rural Rutland was the home of two very distinguished preserved engines. Access to the outside world was via various mineral lines, across the remains of the M&GN at South Witham and then via further mineral lines through Buckminster and Stainby to the head of the BR High Dyke mineral line at Colsterworth, thence to the East Coast main line at High Dyke Junction. Here one of the pair, *Pendennis Castle*, undergoes steam tests at Market Overton shed on 3 March 1974.

Above:
The other famous inmate, *Flying Scotsman*, has left Colsterworth and is about to cross the A1 road on the High Dyke branch on her way out from Market Overton on 29 March 1974.

Above left:
Class 02/2 2-8-0 No 63936 of Grantham approaches the top end of the High Dyke branch near Colsterworth having hauled her empty wagons up the steep bank on 14 January 1951.

Left:
Class 02/4 2-8-0 No 63932 of Grantham lifts a train of ore empties up High Dyke branch on 13 July 1963.

Above:
At the bottom end of the High Dyke, very early in the morning of 1 April 1974. *Pendennis Castle* exchanges crews before passing by High Dyke box and onto the East Coast main line on the right. She then proceeded to Gloucester. I believe she only returned to Market Overton once more after this before the depot closed down.

Below:
Class 02/2 2-8-0 No 63940 of Grantham lifts a train of ore empties for the High Dyke up the main line through Great Ponton cutting on 23 April 1959.

Above:
Class B12/3 4-6-0 No 61541 of Grantham makes a vigorous start from home with a Skegness-bound excursion on 26 March 1951.

Right:
Class J1 0-6-0 No 65007 of Colwick arrives at Grantham with a train from Derby on 7 April 1950.

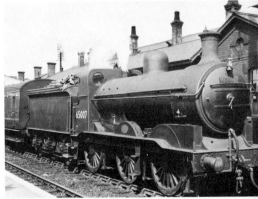

Above:
An unidentified 'B1' 4-6-0 lifts its safety valves impatiently as it waits for the level crossing gates with a Cleethorpes-King's Cross express on 22 December 1952.

Left:
Class C12 4-4-2T No 67350 the pioneer of the class at home on Boston shed on 27 April 1952.

Below:
A 'Ragtimer' Class K2 No 61760 poses outside her home shed at Boston on 27 April 1952.

Above left:
'B1' class 4-6-0 No 61405 of Lincoln passes
Stickney station on the cross-country line to
Firsby Junction and Skegness with an express for
the seaside on 6 July 1952.

Left:
Side-window cab Class K2 2-6-0 No 61729 of
Colwick takes the south to east leg of the Firsby
triangle with a Skegness-bound weekend special
on 6 September 1952. The north to east side of
the triangle swings away to the station on the
right whilst the Grimsby-Peterborough main line
forming the base runs across in the background.

Above:
Class K3 2-6-0 No 61809 of Gorton gains the
Skegness branch at Firsby East Junction with a
Skegness train on 6 September 1952.

Right:
'K3' class 2-6-0 No 61816 of Colwick passes
Seacroft on the outskirts of Skegness with a
return summer weekend special to
Burton-on-Trent on 6 September 1952.

Below:
Skegness station on 19 July 1953 with Class K2 2-6-0 No 61780 of Colwick getting ready to leave with a return excursion.

Below:
Class K2 2-6-0 No 61747 of Colwick storms through Burgh-le-Marsh on 6 September 1952 with a summer weekend special for Mablethorpe. She will leave the main line at Willoughby to gain the Mablethorpe loop.

Derby

Above:
Black Five No 44888 of Saltley comes past Derby station north box with an up express for Birmingham and the southwest on 10 March 1963.

Right:
GC 'Director' No 62663 *Prince Albert* of Doncaster at Derby Midland with a Lincoln train on 16 September 1954.

Above:
GN Class N1 0-6-2T No 69481 of Colwick at Nottingham Victoria on 20 January 1955 with a train from Basford.

Left:
SR 'Schools' class 4-4-0 No 30925 *Cheltenham* at Nottingham Victoria on 13 May 1962. She is piloting LMS Class 2 4-4-0 No 40646 on an RCTS special to Darlington.

Above right:
LTS 4-4-2T No 41943 of Mansfield at Nottingham Midland on 29 June 1952. The overbridge carrying the GC main line over the station can just be seen at top left.

Right:
The only 'K2' 2-6-0 with a side-window cab operating south of the Border, No 61729 of Colwick at her home shed on 30 June 1952.

Below:
LMS 'Jubilee' 4-6-0 No 45568 *Western Australia* of Leeds takes water beside Nottingham Station East box on 27 January 1955 with a St Pancras express via Melton and Oakham.

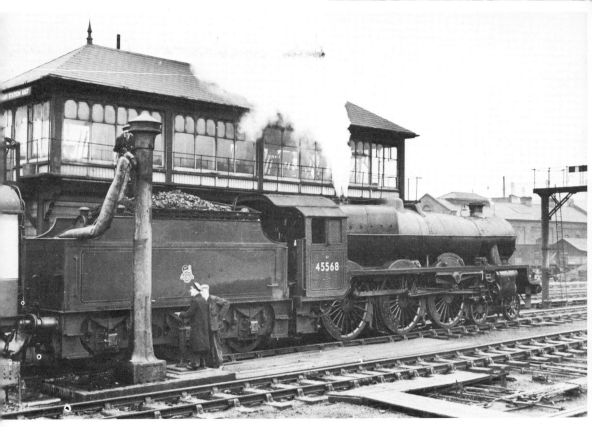

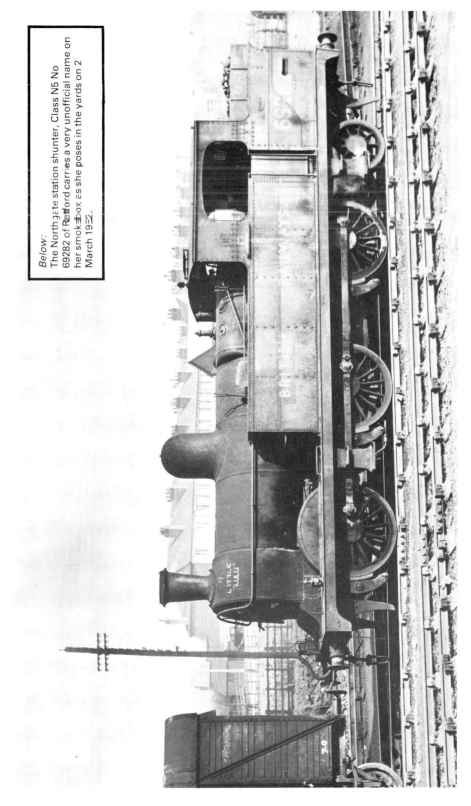

Below:
The Northgate station shunter, Class N5 No 69282 of Retford carries a very unofficial name on her smokebox as she poses in the yards on 2 March 1952.

Right:
MR Class 1F 0-6-0T No 41686 of Nottingham in the small two-road Midland shed at Lincoln St Marks alongside a Johnson Class 2 4-4-0 on 29 July 1951.

Below:
Class B16/3 4-6-0 No 61448 of York heads for the bottleneck of the level crossing over Lincoln High Street out of the Central station with a Yarmouth-York express which she has just taken over on 20 May 1949.

Above:
This church alongside Lincoln Central station's High Street box at the northern exit to the station must on occasions have suffered from unholy 'noises off' during services although GC Class J11 No 64303 is running past very quietly as she comes off her home shed, on 20 May 1949.

Below:
'Footballer' Class B17/4 4-6-0 No E1667 *Bradford* runs into the Central station with a down stopping train on 20 May 1949. According to my record she was a Woodford engine.

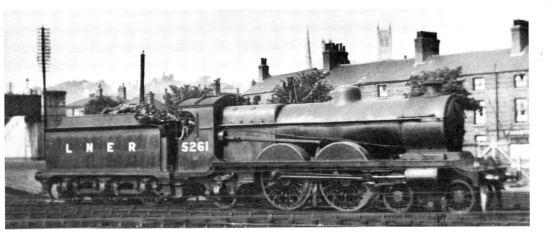

Left:
A prewar picture of Lincoln Central with GC 'Glenalmond' Class B9 4-6-0 No 5280 pausing to take water with a Skegness-bound excursion.

Below left:
Class 02/1 2-8-0 No 63930 of Grantham runs through Central station with an up coal train on 20 May 1949.

Above:
A GC Class C4 'Jersey Lily' No 5261 shows off her graceful lines as she backs down from the GC shed into Lincoln Central in this prewar picture. The towers of Lincoln Cathedral are in the background.

Below:
Another prewar picture, GC 'Director' No 5503 (later 62667) *Somme* runs off shed into the down side of Central station.

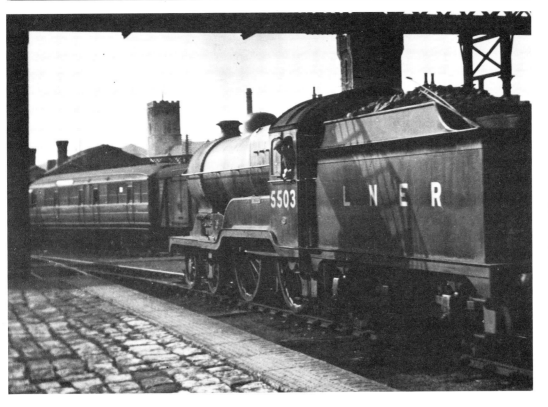

Above:
Class K3 2-6-0 No 61806 of Gorton passes Five Mile House with an excursion for Skegness. A bleak spot on a bleak day, 16 July 1950.

Right:
Class A1/1 Pacific No 60113 *Great Northern* of New England approaches Five Mile House with the down special from King's Cross to York to celebrate the centenary of the opening of the route on 16 July 1950.

Below:
Class J11 No 64320 of Louth arrives at Bardney with a pick up freight from Louth on 13 October 1951.

Above:
GN Class C12 4-4-2T No 67379 of Boston at East Barkwith with a Bardney-Louth train on 13 October 1951.

Left:
No 67379 again passing through Benninworth Haven with a Louth-Bardney train on 13 October 1951.

Left:
The ornate portico of Louth station on 22 April 1970.

Below:
GN Class D2 4-4-0 No 2164 of Boston drifts into Louth station with a down freight on 16 May 1949. 'C12' No 67364 is on a Mablethorpe loop train behind.

Right:
GC Class A5 4-6-2T No 9817 of Doncaster shunts wagons in the station on 18 May 1949.

Below right:
GC Class A5 4-6-2T No 69810 of Boston runs through the station with an up freight on 18 May 1949.

Left:
Across the flat lands of the Lincolnshire Marshes Class C12 4-4-2T No 67398 of Louth brings a Willoughby-Louth train into Sutton-on-Sea on 21 July 1953.

Below:
GC Class A5 4-6-2T No 69803 of Louth pauses at Mablethorpe with a Louth-Willoughby train of GN flat roofed four-wheel and articulated stock 24 September 1954.

Right:
Ex MSL Class N5 0-6-2T No 69306 of Louth leaves Theddlethorpe for Mablethorpe on 4 September 1952.

Below:
No miles to nowhere!
Once upon a time this milepost stood against the busy signalbox of Saxby station junction, the western end of the M&GN System, now, on 3 May 1975 it stands alone in empty waste ground – symbolic perhaps of what has happened to so much of the railway network east of the Midlands.